10 Tips For Using Pinterest For Your Family History & Genealogy

MELISSA DICKERSON,
GENEALOGY GIRL TALKS

I0424078

Copyright © 2016 Melissa Dickerson, Genealogy Girl Talks

All rights reserved.

ISBN: 153471068X
ISBN-13: 978-1534710689

Any trademarks, service marks, product names or named features are the property of their respective owners, and are used only for reference. There is no implied endorsement if we use one or any of these logos, terms, and any other copyright and trademark information.

If you received this publication from anyone other than Genealogy Girl Talks, you've received a pirated copy. Please contact us via e-mail at genealogygirltalks@gmail.com and notify us of the situation.

Please note that much of this publication is based on personal experience and anecdotal evidence. Although the author and publisher have made every reasonable attempt to achieve complete accuracy of the content in this eBook file, they assume no responsibility for errors or omissions. Also, you should use this information as you see fit, and at your own risk. Your particular situation may not be exactly suited to the examples illustrated here; in fact, it's likely that they won't be the same, and you should adjust your use of the information and recommendations accordingly.

Finally, keep in mind that nothing in this book is intended to replace common sense, legal, medical or other professional advice, and is only meant to inform and entertain the reader. So have fun with the **10 Tips for Searching The Find A Grave Website For Your Family History & Genealogy**.

Copyright © 2016 Melissa Dickerson, Genealogy Girl Talks (a division of RMJET, LLC). All rights reserved worldwide.

DEDICATION

My family who continually support me in each of my endeavors.
I love you all!

CONTENTS

I put together this short little guide to help you use Pinterest for your Family History and Genealogy. It is filled with brief tips to help you in this journey!

Keep in mind that there is no right or wrong way to use Pinterest for your Family History. The beauty of Pinterest is that it is completely customizable and you can tweak it as you go!

I hope these 10 Tips help you as you begin to use Pinterest for your Family History & Genealogy!

Have fun with it!

Happy Pinning!

1 PINTEREST IS A SEARCH ENGINE

Keep in mind that Pinterest is considered a search engine. Keywords and searchable terms are necessary to be found. How can you use these keywords? Place keywords such as Family Surnames in the pin description of your pins. This will help others find you!

2 COMPLETE YOUR PROFILE

Be sure to completely fill out your Pinterest profile. Complete your "About Me" section to assist others in finding you! Remember to use keywords (see above) in your description. If you have a blog or website, add that information to your profile, too!

3 CONSIDER USING TEMPLATES

Keep in mind that if a website has a "pin it" button they are giving you permission to use and "pin" their images to Pinterest. On the flip-side, if they do not have a "pin it" button they are technically not giving permission to pin their images. Now I know there are a lot of websites that do not understand Pinterest, or the importance of using Pinterest, but to comply with copyrights consider using a Template for images and links to websites.

4 PIN IT & SHARE

Did you know that you can share your pins on other social media sites? Facebook, Twitter, and more allow you to integrate your pins. Consider using these to share your pins (and help others find you).

5 USE THE DIRECT MESSAGING SERVICE

This is a new service offered by Pinterest and I believe it is a valuable tool to connecting with family!

6 COMMENT ON PINS

Commenting on pins can start a conversation! You never know the family you will meet just by commenting!

7 FOLLOW OTHERS

This is a mistake I made in the beginning of my Pinterest journey: I didn't follow others. Now, I've learned the importance of following other "pinners". I don't follow so they will "follow me back" but I follow to find more pins for my own boards!

8 FILL IN YOUR BOARD DESCRIPTIONS

Your board descriptions help people find your boards on Pinterest. Remember Pinterest is a search engine and users can search for information by boards. You want to make sure your board descriptions are completed and contain keywords (or search terms) that others will use to find you!

9 THE MORE, THE MERRIER

In my own journey using Pinterest for Genealogy I have found that the more pins on a board, the more views I receive. I'm not sure how this happens, but for some reason it does. So, I would suggest that you fill your boards with a lot of quality pins!

10 CHECK THE LINKS

How do you check the link of your pins? A simple "click-through" will check the destination URL (or website) of the pin. This will help your followers! Do you want to send your followers to a spammy website through one of the pins you pinned to your boards? Take a quick second to make sure the pin sends people to the correct website.

11 BONUS TIP #1

Make sure the pin description is filled out! I've seen many users that simply have a "." or the words "love" as their pin description. This will make it difficult for your pins (and you) to be found on Pinterest. Take a moment to fill in the pin descriptions located under the pin.

12 BONUS TIP #2

Use the Secret Boards that Pinterest provides. There are several ways to use the Secret Boards. For example, when you are creating a new board and you only have a few pins added you can create a secret board to fill up and then make it visible to others. Or you can add pins to your secret board and then repin them to a public board. Consider using your Secret Boards - they can really come in handy!

13 BONUS TIP #3

Remember that the order in which you pin your pins is the order they appear on your boards. Does that sound a little confusing? Basically it means your older pins are at the bottom of the board and the newest ones are at the top. If you want a few of your pins to appear together on your board, consider using the Secret Boards and then repin them to your public board in your predetermined order.

ABOUT THE AUTHOR

 Melissa Dickerson, also known as "Genealogy Girl Talks" has been conducting family history and genealogy research for over twenty years. She has a love of history, family, teaching, and creativity. Those four passions pushed her to create Genealogy Girl Talks in 2014.

She wrote her first eBook, "10 Tips for Using Pinterest for Family History" in the Fall 2014. That was followed by several more quick tip eBooks. In May 2016, her first print book was self-published ("Using Pinterest for Family History and Genealogy").

Melissa lives in Northeast Ohio, but her roots find her deep in pursuit of her family history in Appalachia. Her burning desire to learn more about her family and her roots in Southwestern West Virginia has quickly become her life's pursuit.

www.ingramcontent.com/pod-product-compliance
Lightning Source LLC
Chambersburg PA
CBHW062029280526
45787CB00005B/2254